Colors in Nature

Green

by Martha E. H. Rustad

Ideas for Parents and Teachers

Bullfrog Books let children practice reading informational text at the earliest reading levels. Repetition, familiar words, and photo labels support early readers.

Before Reading

- Discuss the cover photo. What does it tell them?
- Look at the picture glossary together. Read and discuss the words.

Read the Book

- "Walk" through the book and look at the photos. Let the child ask questions. Point out the photo labels.
- Read the book to the child, or have him or her read independently.

After Reading

- Prompt the child to think more. Ask: What green things do you see outside? Are they natural or man-made?

For Leif, as green was once your favorite color.
—MEHR

Bullfrog Books are published by Jump!
5357 Penn Avenue South
Minneapolis, MN 55419
www.jumplibrary.com

Library of Congress Cataloging-in-Publication Data
Rustad, Martha E. H. (Martha Elizabeth Hillman), 1975-
  Green / by Martha E.H. Rustad.
    pages cm. -- (Colors in nature)
  Summary: "This photo-illustrated book for early readers tells about plants, animals, and how green works in the natural world. Includes picture glossary"-- Provided by publisher.
  Includes bibliographical references and index.
  ISBN 978-1-62031-039-7 (hardcover : alk. paper)
  ISBN 978-1-62496-037-6 (ebook)
  1. Color in nature--Juvenile literature. 2. Green--Juvenile literature. I. Title.
  QC495.5.R87 2014
  535.6--dc23   2012039680

Series Editor   Rebecca Glaser
Book Designer   Ellen Huber
Photo Researcher   Heather Dreisbach

Photo Credits: Dreamstime, 9, 20, 23tl, 23mr; Shutterstock, cover, 1, 3t, 3b, 5, 6, 7, 8, 10, 11, 12, 13, 14, 15, 18, 19, 21, 22a, 22b, 22c, 22d, 23ml, 23bl, 23tr, 23br, 24; Superstock, 4, 17

Printed in the United States of America at Corporate Graphics, North Mankato, Minnesota.
4-2013 / PO 1003

10 9 8 7 6 5 4 3 2 1

Table of Contents

Green All Around

What things are green?
Look around in nature.

I see a green tomato.
Why is it green?
It is not ripe yet.

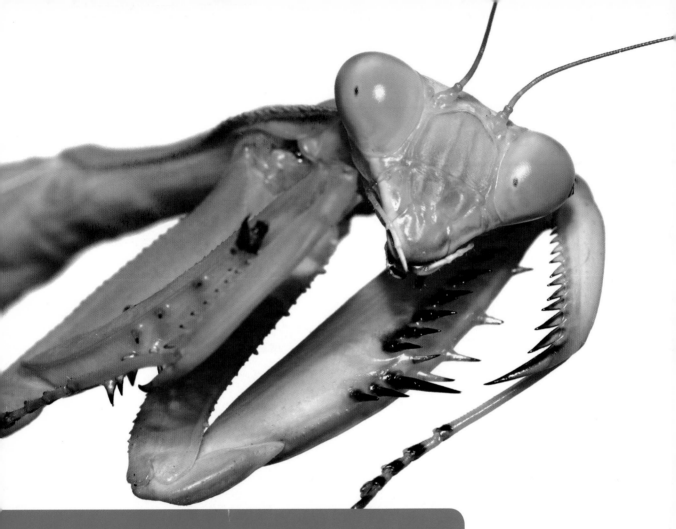

I see a praying mantis.
Why is it green?

Its color helps it
hide near plants.

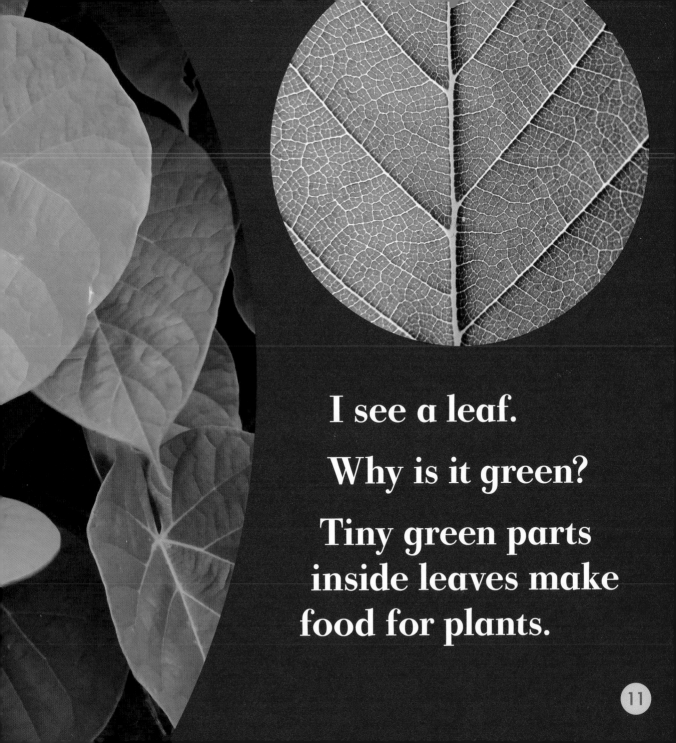

I see a leaf.

Why is it green?

Tiny green parts inside leaves make food for plants.

I see an evergreen tree.
Why is it green?

Its needles make food
for the tree all year.

I see a frog.
Why is it green?

Green hides frogs in ponds.

I see a chameleon.
Why is it green?
It changes color
when it is scared.

feather

I see a parakeet.

Why is it green?

Green feathers
hide it from
other animals.

I see a sloth.
Why is it green?
Algae grow
on its fur.

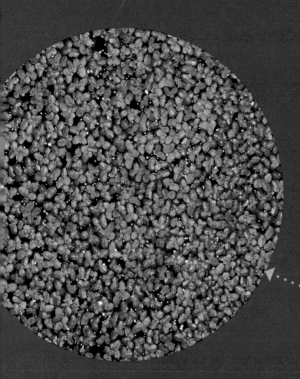

algae

Where do you see green?

21

Shades of Green

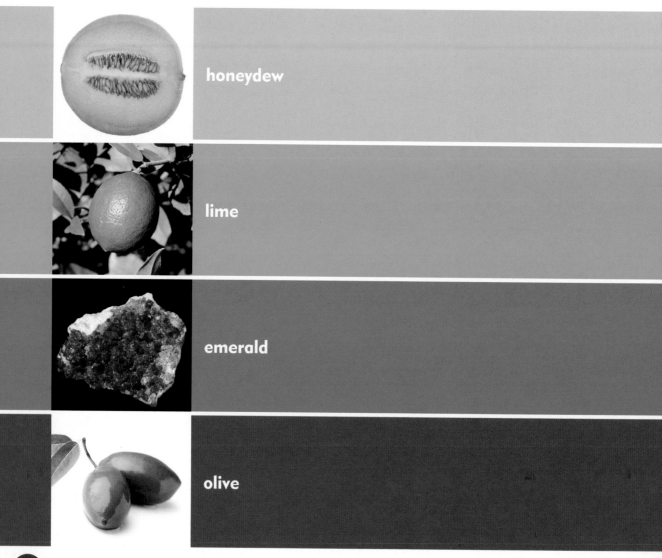

honeydew

lime

emerald

olive

Picture Glossary

algae
Small plants with no roots or stems that grow in wet places.

parakeet
A small kind of parrot, with a long tail.

chameleon
A small lizard with a long tail; chameleons can change the color of their skin.

praying mantis
An insect that looks like it is praying when it folds its front legs.

needle
A leaf on an evergreen tree.

sloth
A slow-moving mammal with long arms and legs that lives in rainforest trees.

Index

To Learn More

Learning more is as easy as 1, 2, 3.

1) Go to www.factsurfer.com

2) Enter "green" into the search box.

3) Click the "Surf" button to see a list of websites.

With factsurfer.com, finding more information is just a click away."